Your Best Selfie

Motivations to help you achieve your potential in the age of Instagram, Tik Tok, and other time wasters

By

Jonathan Robinette M.Ed

You have the brains you need.

You have the strength.

You have the drive.

You have grit.

Those traits already live inside of you.

However, they can only be activated by you.

Identify your goal.

Stay focused.

Find a way.

Not an excuse.

"Without effort, your talent is nothing more than unmet potential. Without effort, your skill is nothing more than what you could have done but didn't."

-Angela Duckworth

Today more than ever, it is essential to understand that strength of character and accomplishment can only come from embracing *struggle*, that it is necessary to *suffer* through laborious tasks, and that answers to tough questions often do not come as easily as Google searches or Siri requests.

Once struggle is embraced, anything is possible.

The human brain is designed to do *WORK*. Hard work. Arduous work. At times even boring work. Don't shy away from it.

Pursue it!

"It's better to aim high and miss than to aim low and hit"

-Les Brown

Set goals for yourself that are realistic, but outside of your comfort zone. I set a goal for myself, *every year* to read 100 books. I've never achieved that goal. The closest I've come is 82 books in one year. But, if I would have set my goal to 50 books or even 60, I probably would have reached that goal and then stopped soon after.

Setting your goals high will allow you to exceed your own expectations.

"Strength is a product of struggle. You must do what others won't to achieve what others don't"

-Henry Rollins

Do not run from difficulty. Embrace it. Whether it is academics, athletics, or personal achievement, you will not improve unless you push yourself out of your comfort zone.

"He (or she) who says he can, and he who says he can't are both usually right"

-Confucius

Nothing could be more beneficial to you than eliminating the word *"can't"* from your vocabulary. Turn down the volume on your negative self- talk. Eliminate it altogether. Don't allow negativity to infect your mind and crush your dreams. Tap into the power of auto-suggestion.

Talk to *yourself* the way you would talk to your closest friend who was having a bad day.

*"It ain't about how hard you can hit, it's about how hard you can **get hit** and keep moving forward. It's about how much you can take and keep moving forward. That's how winning is done!"*

-Sylvester Stallone
From the movie "Rocky Balboa"

In life, you will fail. You will fail more often than you would like.

To succeed, you will need to build *resilience,* the inner strength necessary to recover quickly from life's difficulties.

To build resilience, Kenneth Ginsberg MD suggests employing the Seven C's:

- *Control:* Set goals that are not dependent on others.

- *Confidence:* When you build skills through repeated and deliberate practice, your confidence will increase.

- *Coping:* You will have setbacks. Knowing that failure is a necessary part of improvement will help you keep it in perspective.

- *Competence*: Practice, practice, practice!

- *Character*: Follow your moral compass.

- *Contribution*: Share your skills. Offer to teach your expertise to others.

- *Connection:* Become a part of a community of others who share similar goals, challenges, and creative solutions.

"If you really want something, you'll find a way. If you don't, you'll find an excuse.

-Jim Rohn

Your position in life, good or bad, will be an accumulation of the choices *you* make.

Don't blame your parents or your teachers, your social status, your gender, or your race.

Eliminate excuses.

It is up to you to write the story of your life.

"As you think, so shall you become"

-Bruce Lee

When you talk to yourself, choose your words wisely.

The imagination becomes material.

Your thoughts will become your reality.

"*Seek first to understand, then to be understood*"

-Stephen Covey

I had a student a few years ago. He was a good student, very bright and well liked by the others in the class. One day he started talking in class. A lot. Over a few weeks, his talking turned to defiance. He got detentions from me and other teachers at school.

One day, after I witnessed a rather nasty barb directed toward another student, I pulled him into the hallway.

"What is your problem?! You used to be such a good student!" I was firm and direct. He didn't respond. "The last month you have been a horrible disruption in not only my class, but all of your others!" He stood without saying a word. His eyes filled with tears and he stared at me. When he finally spoke, I felt like I had been punched in the stomach.

"My mom was put in prison last month."

This explained his behavior. Not surprisingly, my relationship with him changed after that. Once I and his other teachers *understood* his challenges, we were able to put in place a multi layered system of assistance with his teachers, counselors and the administration so that he could return to being the student he was capable of being.

*"I have learned that the opposite of cruelty is not simply the freedom from the cruel relationship; it is **hospitality**"*

-Phillip Hallie

"Tolerance", "acceptance", and even "kindness" are all, in my opinion, overused and empty words that give lip service to the way we want others to live, but do very little to positively impact the lives of others.

Hospitality, on the other hand, requires action. Hospitality requires *sacrifice*.

Hospitality is going out of your way for the benefit of someone else, someone you may not even know, with no expectation of personal gain, while at the same time sacrificing your time, money, personal freedom, or even social status.

"*People are rewarded in public for what they practice for years in private.*"

-Tony Robbins

No one is born just "good" at something. There is no such thing as a "prodigy".

The fifth grader who can play Mozart on the piano, the kindergarten black belt, the best ball handler on the soccer team, and the ballet dancer on pointe before her tenth birthday all share commonalities: they set specific goals, remained laser focused, and spent hours and hours laboring on their craft.

You can do the same.

"If you persuade yourself that you can do a certain thing, provided this thing be possible, you will do it, however difficult it may be. If, on the contrary, you imagine that you cannot do the simplest thing in the world, it is impossible for you to do it, and molehills become for you unscalable mountains."

-Emile Coue

Even if you think it may be *impossible*, your hard work can make it a reality.

A year ago during class, I mentioned this to my students. One boy in the back, thinking he could easily disprove the ambitious claim, raised his hand and asked, "What about flying, Mr. R? No person can fly! It's impossible!" Many of the kids nodded in silent agreement.

I showed the class video of British inventor Richard Browning and his Iron Man-like flying suit and Gary Connery's 2,500ft jump from a helicopter without a parachute.

At once, the seemingly impossible became possible.

"Talent is Overrated"

-Geoff Colvin

Talent does not come from being born with a natural or unfair advantage. Talent only comes from inner fire, hours of deliberate practice, avoiding time wasters, and starting early in life (although it is *never* too late to start!)

In a response to journalists who often claimed he was born possessing an innate basketball ability, Michael Jordan, perhaps the greatest of all time, responded in an advertisement by saying: *"Maybe I led you to believe that basketball was God-given gift and not something I worked for, every single day of my life."*

"I hated every minute of training, but I said 'Don't quit! Suffer now and live the rest of your life as a champion."

-Muhammad Ali

You choose what your life will look like when you're an adult. Do the hard things now and your life will be easy. Do the easy things now and well, get comfortable flipping burgers in your thirties.

Do the hard things early in life and *EVERY DAY*.

- Study more,

- Get up early,

- Break up with your phone,

- Push yourself physically,

- Eat more plants,

- Eat less junk,

- Read challenging books,

- Practice an instrument,

- Write down your goals,

- Stay focused!

"It does not matter how slowly you go as long as you do not stop."

-Confucious

The Japanese call it "Kaizen." I call it, *the accumulation of nominal gains."*

Small, consistent changes over time will add up to massive improvement. Each day, these changes may be barely perceptible but, done continually, will lead to endless growth.

Think Big. Dream bigger. But, start small.

"Surround yourself with O.Q.P. 'Only Quality People.'

-Les Brown

Your success in life depends on the kind of people you associate with.

If you want to be a better student, you should make friends with the kids who already have academic honors. If your dream is to be a millionaire and start your own business, join a youth entrepreneurs club and surround yourself with likeminded people. Is it your dream to write the next great American novel? Join a writer's workshop!

Low achieving friends will be your biggest advocates for your low achieving life.

Associating with O.Q.P. will pave the way to higher achievement.

"Effort and attitude are the only tools necessary for success."

-Jonathan Robinette

Harvard transcripts, rich parents, being born tall and beautiful can all provide a distinct advantage early on.

Ultimately, however, it is the people with the best attitude who are willing to outwork others who will dominate the pack.

Show up early, leave a little late, and do it with a smile on your face.

*"Don't prepare. Begin. Our enemy is not lack of preparation. The enemy is **resistance**, our chattering brain producing excuses. Start before you are ready."*

-Steven Pressfield

The biggest enemy you have to deal with lives inside you.

When you would rather scroll on your phone than study, or post to your IG story instead of practice, or binge watch Netflix rather than challenge your mind, that is your enemy working against you.

The enemy's name is *Resistance*.

Resistance will tell you anything to keep you from achieving your greatness.

Fight Resistance.

Always.

"I fully realize that no wealth or position can long endure, unless built upon truth and justice, therefore, I will engage in no transaction that does not benefit all whom it affects."

-Napoleon Hill

Cheating, stealing, lying, backstabbing - they may advance someone's position *momentarily*, but their gains eventually will subside.

Failure will always take place.

I have an acquaintance to whom I loaned a significant sum of money to start a business. After the business launched to surprising success, he decided to keep the money for himself and refused to talk to me or the other investor.

We watched in bitter disbelief as the business grew and was promoted on TV and in magazine articles.

We spent thousands of dollars on lawyers to get our money back as he lived a "good life".

A year later the business had failed. He was unemployed, bankrupt, and drug addicted.

"When the mind goes negative, the mouth goes positive."

-Kevin Bracy

Self talk is the internal dialogue that is influenced by your subconscious mind. It is the repetitive thoughts, beliefs, or ideas that, positive or negative, will ultimately become your reality.

If you can change the way you talk to yourself, you can change your life.

When your mind starts to ruminate on failures, inadequacies, or disabilities, use positive affirmations to reprogram your negative subconscious.

42

"When we help ourselves, we find moments of happiness. When we help others, we find lasting fulfillment."

-Simon Sinek

If you are not making someone else's life better, then you are wasting your time.

True happiness and achievement come from giving and helping, not the accumulation of material possessions.

Giving and helping are hospitable acts. Hospitality requires sacrifice.

What are you prepared to do?

"Be so good they can't ignore you."

-Cal Newport

I've had students who have wanted to be first chair trumpet, or wished they could be the starting quarterback or hoped that they could get straight A's. Hoping, wanting and wishing are not plans of *action*.

It takes massive action and consistent dedication to achieve any of those goals.

But, if you're willing to step up, stay focused and outwork the next person, your effort will be rewarded.

You will not be ignored.

"The act of taking the first step is what separates the winners from the losers."

-Brian Tracy

Accomplishments only come through *movement*; small, consistent changes in a positive direction.

The sum of that movement is momentum.

Momentum will create growth.

Growth will lead to achievement.

Start by taking your first step today. Just make sure you continue every day!

"If you have trouble sleeping at night, you didn't work hard enough that day."

-My dad, Ed Robinette

The human body is designed to solve problems, outdoors, in nearly constant motion. Unfortunately, kids today are getting less outdoor activity while spending way too much time hypnotized by the blue light of a screen.

It's no surprise that students have a hard time falling asleep, getting up in the morning, and staying awake in class.

Put down your phone. Step away from the TV and computer. Go outside!

Challenge yourself physically.

Ever.

Single.

Day.

"My advice to the youth is in 4 P's: perceive, prepare, perform, and persevere."

-Brigadier General Charles McGee

100 years old

Member of the Tuskegee Airmen

The Tuskegee Airmen were the first African American military pilots to successfully complete their training and enter the Army Air Corps (Army Air Forces).

Perceive: Understand what you are meant to do and why it is important.

Prepare: Get educated. Identify your goal. Make its' pursuit a daily habit.

Perform: Strive for excellence.

Persevere: Entertain no excuses. Fight resistance.

"If you want to change the world, you must be your very best in the darkest moments."

-Admiral William McRraven

US Special Operations Command

Navy SEAL Team 6

Life will be difficult and at times you will fail.

If you are like most people, you will fail *often*.

Get over it. That is just the way life is and many times it is out of your control.

What you can control is your *reaction* to the adversities you will invariable face.

Will you take control, accept responsibility, use failure to learn from mistakes and an opportunity for growth?

Or, will you blame someone? Will you look to mom and dad to "fix" it? Will you cower? Will you shy away from discomfort when your back is to the wall?

54

"Hustle beats talent when talent doesn't hustle."

-Unknown

Actions breed results.

Some are born with an innate advantage that starts them closer to the finish line: a petite frame suitable for an Olympic gymnast, the height and wingspan of a power forward, or the long, tapered fingers of a concert pianist.

Natural gifts are useless without the hunger to build, to create, and to achieve.

Hustle allowed *five foot seven* Spud Webb to win the NBA slam dunk contest. Hustle made legless Jennifer Bricker the first handicapped state tumbling champion. And, stricken with a debilitating neurological disease, hustle pushed Kayla Montgomery to become North Carolina state cross country champion.

"I do not fear problems, I solve them. I do not ignore problems, I confront them. I do not avoid problems, I conquer them."

-Shad Helmstetter

Inside of every problem is the key to its solution.

Don't view problems as your enemy. Problems are challenges that offer an opportunity to learn, to grow, and to mature.

Attack them! Don't shy away from them.

You will only improve by living inside your *discomfort* zone.

"Don't make a habit out of choosing what feels good over what's actually good for you."

-Eric Thomas

Social media is not good for you. *Period.*

It's easy. It is a time waster.

It is highly addictive.

Instagram "likes" affect your brain's reward area the same way as other destructive substances such as cocaine, alcohol, and nicotine.

Like cigarettes and booze, social media offers a momentary high, but can destroy emotional connections to others.

It feels good. But, it is not good for you.

Delete your accounts and spend that formerly wasted time developing skills and knowledge you can take with you for a lifetime.

"If your life were a book and you were the author, how would you want the story to go?"

-Amy Purdy

It's terrifying.

It's humbling.

It's confusing.

Because, let's face it, it's all up to *you*!

It is your responsibility to write the book of your life. You're the author. You decide how the story ends.

Don't fear it, celebrate it.

And, get to work!

"How wonderful it is that nobody need wait a single moment before starting to improve the world."

-Anne Frank

Improvement requires change.

Change can be scary; fear and intimidation often rise from the unknown.

You may choose to fight change or embrace it.

Either way, change is *inevitable*.

You can affect change through your reaction to it, and more importantly, your initiation of it.

Be the change that you wish to see in your world.

"Your attitude, not your aptitude, will determine your altitude."

-Zig Ziglar

Even the very best are expendable.

There is a long line of professional athletes, actors, and musicians who threw away millions of dollars because their talent was without character.

No matter how hard you worked, no matter how good you've become, your teammates, your coaches, and even your friends will eventually turn their backs to you if your attitude is toxic.

A bad attitude is like a flat tire, you won't get very far until you change it!

"Fear is part of everything you do...you have to take great risks to get big rewards."

-Greg Louganis

It's OK to be afraid. *Everyone* experiences fear.

Fear of failure and fear of success are common but so is the fear of disappointing others, the fear of the future, and social fears.

Fear builds to crippling proportions when it is fed and nurtured by *you*. Therefore, fear exists only in the mind.

You control fear. It doesn't control you.

You *can* face it.

You *can* push past it.

You *will* destroy it.

"Reading is to the mind, as exercise is to the body."

-Brian Tracy

Never stop pushing yourself mentally or physically. A sound body needs depends upon a sound mind. They should not exist as separate entities.

Challenge yourself physically and *read* each and every day. Required homework, reading social media posts, magazines and comics do not count.

Get a book. A challenging book. A book that is written just above your current level, is longer than you've ever read before, and about which you know nothing.

Do this for at least one hour every day, for the rest of your life.

"If you fail and people laugh at you, they're not worth your time. Ignore them."

-Gary Vaynerchuk

When some others see you advancing, they will be intimidated. They will be envious. They will celebrate your setbacks to make themselves feel better.

Do not worry about what others will say. Waste not time worrying what they think. You cannot control how they feel.

Stay true to yourself, to your relentless pursuit of your passion, and to the people who are cheering you on.

"Imagine if you will being on your deathbed. And, standing around your bed – the ghosts of the ideas, the dreams, the abilities, the talents given to you by life. And that you, for whatever reason, you never acted on those ideas, you never pursued that dream, you never used those talents, we never saw your leadership, you never used your voice, you never wrote that book.

And there they are standing around your bed looking at you with large angry eyes saying we came to you! And, only you could have given us life! Now we must die with you forever. The question is – if you die today what ideas, what dreams, what abilities, what talents, what gifts, would die with you? "

– Les Brown

There are words you must write, songs you will sing, art you will create, and games you will win. They live inside *you*. Don't underestimate their importance. Don't deny us their significance.

Let them out. Give them life, as only you can. Do not let them die in stagnation.

You owe it to the people who believed in you. You owe it to your friends, your teachers, your coaches, and your parents. You owe it to the people who doubted you and celebrated your failures.

You owe it to the world.

"*No whining. No complaining. No excuses.*"

-Angela Duckworth

75

Enough said.